VAMPIRE BATS

By the Same Author

Animals and Their Niches
Frost Hollows and Other Microclimates
The Minnow Family
Natural Fire

VAMPIRE BATS

Laurence Pringle

illustrated with photographs

William Morrow and Company
New York   1982

Printed in the United States of America.
1 2 3 4 5 6 7 8 9 10

Library of Congress Cataloging in Publication Data

Pringle, Laurence P.
  Vampire bats.

  Includes index.
  Summary: Describes the behavior of three species of small blood-eating bats of the leafnose family found in Mexico, Central America, and South America.
  1. Vampire bats—Juvenile literature. [1. Vampire bats. 2. Bats] I. Title.
QL737.C52P74   599.4   81-16897
ISBN 0-688-01083-0   AACR2
ISBN 0-688-01085-7 (lib. bdg.)

Permission is gratefully acknowledged for the use of the following photographs: J. Scott Altenbach, pp. 4, 28, 29, 38, 39; Denver Wildlife Research Center, U.S. Fish and Wildlife Service, pp. 19, 24, 27, 35, 43, 50, 52, 53 top and bottom; *Movie Star News,* pg. 12; Janet Ross, Cincinnati Zoo, pg. 32; Dennis C. Turner, pp. 25, 34, 41, 44, 45; Gerald S. Wilkinson, pg. 15

The author wishes to thank
Donald J. Elias,
Denver Wildlife Research Center,
U.S. Fish and Wildlife Service,
and Dennis C. Turner,
Zoology Institute,
University of Zurich,
Switzerland,
for reading the manuscript of this book
and helping to improve its accuracy.

CONTENTS

VAMPIRE BATS

1

MEET
THE REAL
VAMPIRE

The sun has set. As full darkness creeps over the land, the coffin lid opens and a stealthy figure emerges. Tall, gaunt, wrapped in a black cloak, the creature sets off on its nightly quest for fresh human blood. It is a vampire.

Tales of such blood-eating creatures can be traced

The actor Bela Lugosi, as the vampire Count Dracula.

13

back for centuries in China, India, Africa, and Europe. The form and habits of these mythical beings varied, and so did their names. In eastern Europe, however, these blood eaters came to be known as vampires, after the Hungarian *vampir*, which may be based on a Turkish word for *witch*.

Vampire tales are still popular today, and so are vampire films, especially the old *Dracula*. People like scarey stories and like to let their imaginations run wild. But there is not a bit of solid evidence that vampires ever existed.

Long before the vampire myths began, three kinds of blood-eating bats lived in Latin America. The first written accounts of these bats were recorded in 1498, when Columbus landed on the island of Trinidad. In the sixteenth century, Spaniards met blood-eating bats as they explored and conquered Central America and Mexico. They were fascinated and frightened by these creatures. The small bats could slip easily through cracks into homes. They also moved quickly and quietly over the ground or the floor of a place where people slept.

In 1565, an Italian explorer named M. Girolame Benzoni wrote in his journal: "There are many bats which bite people during the night; they are found all along this coast [in what is now Costa Rica]... while I

Vampire bats hang upside down in their roosts.
These bats have identification bands on their forearms.

14

was sleeping they bit the toes of my feet so delicately that I felt nothing, and in the morning I found the sheets and mattresses with so much blood that it seemed I had suffered some great injury."

When reports like this one reached Europe, they made people think of the myths about vampires. The belief grew that vampires could turn at will into bats, then back into human form. As a result, the blood-eating bats of the New World were given the name of vampire. Thus, real animals were named after a mythical creature. This book is about the real animals.

More than a hundred species of bats live in the tropical regions of Mexico, Central America, and South America. The vampire bats are part of a large family called the leafnose bats, named for a leaflike flap of skin on the nose of some species. It is hardly noticeable on vampire bats.

Many thousands of years ago vampire bats lived in what is now the United States. Their fossil skeletons have been found in Florida and in northern California. Now the Earth's climate is cooler, and the vampire bats reach only as far north as northern Mexico, rarely straying across the Texas border. In South America, their range extends to northern Argentina and also along the coast of northern Chile.

Though some early reports of vampire bats claimed

The common vampire bat lives in low elevations throughout the area shown in gray.

UNITED STATES

Atlantic Ocean

MEXICO

Gulf of Mexico

WEST INDIES

Caribbean Sea

BELIZE

TRINIDAD

GUYANA

SURINAM

FRENCH GUIANA

GUATEMALA
EL SALVADOR
HONDURAS
NICARAGUA
COSTA RICA

PANAMA

VENEZUELA

COLOMBIA

ECUADOR

PERU

Pacific Ocean

BRAZIL

BOLIVIA

PARAGUAY

CHILE

ARGENTINA

URUGUAY

Atlantic Ocean

that they were big, they are actually small enough to fit easily on your outstretched hand. They measure only about 75 to 90 millimeters (3 to 3¾ inches) long and weigh only about 30 to 50 grams (1 to 1¾ ounces). They are mostly grayish brown in color.

Two of the three kinds of vampire bats are not very common. Little is known about them, except that both get some of their food from birds. One is called the hairy-legged vampire *(Diphylla ecaudata)*. The other is the white-winged vampire *(Diaemus youngi)*.

In 1980, two biologists described how white-winged vampires preyed on chickens, turkeys, and guinea fowl in Brazil. At night, these farm birds roosted on the limbs of trees in a mango orchard. When a white-winged vampire found a roosting bird, it landed nearby and crouched quietly for a while. Then the bat crept to the underside of the limb on which the bird perched and crawled slowly toward its sleeping prey.

Staying on the underside of the limb, the vampire stretched up to bite gently at the bird's toe or foot. Usually a vampire fed on the bird's blood for many minutes without awakening it. If the bird pecked at the wound, the vampire ducked swiftly beneath the limb. There it waited until the bird settled back to sleep, then returned to its meal.

The third blood-eating bat, which has the scientific name of *Desmodus rotundus,* is the most abundant and widespread. Scientists know much more about this

Vampire bats have large upper incisor teeth
with which they nip a bit of flesh from their prey.

common vampire bat than the other two species, because they are more concerned about its effects on its
main sources of food: cattle, horses, other livestock,
and occasionally people.

Charles Darwin was the first scientist to see a vampire bat, during his voyage as naturalist aboard the
British surveying ship H.M.S. *Beagle*. In 1835, Darwin explored inland from the coast of Chile. He and
his men were camped for the night when a servant

noticed that one of their horses was quite nervous. He investigated and found a vampire bat on the horse's back. Darwin described the wound—"slightly swollen and bloody"—and reported that the horse seemed to suffer no ill effects.

Until the European settlement of Latin America, the common vampire bat preyed on wild mammals. Though it sometimes fed on birds and people, its main source of blood was probably mammals such as monkeys, deer, sloths, opossums, and agoutis. A vampire on its nightly hunt for blood first found, then flew or crept close to the prey while it slept.

Vampires living in wild, unsettled regions of their range still feed this way today. Elsewhere, though, the establishment of ranches and farms, with millions of cows, horses, goats, sheep, and pigs, gave vampire bats almost limitless food. Large volumes of blood were available from rather docile, easy-to-find prey. Why look for a deer in a thicket when there are a thousand cows in the pasture? Wherever livestock were available, vampire bats learned to find and feed on them. In many areas, reports of vampire bites on humans declined.

Nevertheless, people gradually became more worried about vampire bats. The bite of a vampire usually seemed harmless, but sometimes a victim died several days later. Bats were suspected as the cause of death. Some horses, cattle, and other livestock also died after being fed upon by vampires. Finally, about 1920, a

20

scientist in southern Brazil discovered that some vampire bats carried the disease of rabies.

Rabies is caused by a virus. Usually an animal becomes infected when it is bitten by a rabid animal, one that is in the last stages of this usually fatal disease. Once the rabies virus enters the body, it multiplies and spreads, reaching the brain and other parts of the nervous system. This process may take days, weeks, or even months. In the final stages of infection, an animal may seem sleepy and shy, or it may be restless and aggressive. In either case, the victim has rabies virus in its saliva. And the victim usually becomes paralyzed, stops breathing, and dies.

Dogs were once thought to be the main victims and carriers of rabies. Now we know that many wild mammals, including skunks, foxes, and bats, may be infected by it. A rabid vampire can be especially dangerous, though, since it bites other mammals in the normal course of feeding. Also, some infected bats do not die of the disease. They survive and carry the rabies virus in their saliva for months or even years. And almost every night they routinely bite a cow or other mammal.

The incidence of rabies in Latin America varies a lot from year to year, and from place to place. In the 1930s, there was an outbreak in Trinidad, causing the death of eighty-nine people and thousands of cattle. Scientists placed the blame on vampire bats.

The disease is usually fatal. Human victims can be

saved only if they are treated with antirabies vaccine soon after being bitten by a rabid animal. Clearly something had to be done to protect people and farm animals. But what? Decades passed before an effective solution was found. Its success depended upon the gradual collection of knowledge about the secret lives of vampire bats.

2

LIFE IN
A VAMPIRE
ROOST

Dozens of scientists worked over a span of many years in order to learn about the lives of vampire bats. Bats were caught in fine-mesh nets, called "mist nets," that were placed near livestock corrals, at cave entrances, or other places where bats were likely to fly. The captured bats were removed unharmed from the nets, and information such as their age, sex, weight, and measurements was recorded. Sometimes a bat was marked

Nets of very fine twine, called "mist nets" (left), entangle
flying bats so they can be examined by biologists, then let go.
Stream channels (above) are flyways for bats.
Mist nets set across streams catch vampires and other bats.

with an identification tag before being released. Re-
capture of a tagged bat enabled scientists to learn
something about its travels, its time of activity, and its
roosting habits.

Some captured bats were caged in laboratories,
where scientists discovered that they could be kept
alive and healthy on meals of cattle blood from slaugh-
terhouses. (The blood had to be whipped so that it did

25

not clot.) From laboratory studies, biologists learned something about the social behavior of vampires. They also saw closeup views of bats feeding on rabbits and other mammals placed in the bat cages.

Outdoors at night, biologists watched cattle and other livestock to see when and how vampire bats came to feed. The scientists usually covered flashlights or vehicle headlights with red filters or red cellophane, to avoid disturbing the bats. (Red light is virtually invisible to bats and other nocturnal mammals.) Special night-vision telescopes, developed by the United States Army, were also used.

Caves and other roosts where vampire bats spend most of their time were explored too. One scientist described his observations in a Guatemalan cave, which was tall enough to stand in but only two feet wide, in this way: "There was the distinctive odor of vampires, a sickly sweet smell I had noticed in vampire caves in Mexico. Vampires hung from the wall just ahead. Some, disturbed by our entrance, launched themselves with powerful leg thrusts and disappeared down the passage. Others scrambled about the walls as agilely as crabs or spiders, seemingly reluctant to fly. Still others appeared too young to take wing, but jumped to the floor of the shaft and bounded ahead of us, looking for all the world like toads. They hopped

Night-vision telescopes enable biologists
to watch vampire bats approach and feed on cattle.

A high-speed photograph of a common vampire bat in mid jump.

faster than we could follow or disappeared into passages too small for us to enter."

Vampires are the most agile of all bats. In fact, they dart over the ground or other surfaces more quickly than many small rodents. Rearing up on their wrists and feet, they can walk, hop, or run over the ground,

Beginning on a flat surface with folded wings,
a common vampire bat leaps into the air, then spreads its wings.

up a wall, or along the back of a cow. They have exceptionally strong legs. Unlike other bats, vampires do not need to spread their wings before leaping into flight. Vampires jump into the air, then spread their wings. The wing span of an adult is about 38 centimeters (15 inches).

Vampires have better eyesight than many other kinds of bats. Scientists tested their vision in laboratories and concluded that the bats see as well at night as rats. One biologist calculated that a vampire bat should be able to see a cow in a pasture at a distance of 130 meters (429 feet).

Like all bats, vampires emit sounds, some of which are too high-pitched for human hearing. By listening to echoes of these cries reflected from objects ahead of them, flying bats can avoid obstacles and locate prey. This echolocation ability is most highly developed among the kinds of bats that catch insects in the air. Since vampire bats hunt much larger prey, their echolocation ability is much less sensitive.

The calls of vampires are a part of their communication with one another. Sometimes they shriek in a dispute over a feeding spot. When a mother bat returns to the roost where her baby waits, the young bat gives a two-note cry and the mother calls back. These special sounds may help the mother distinguish her youngster from others and maintain the strong bond between mother and young.

Usually a female vampire has just one offspring.

Baby vampire bats are born naked except for some short hairs on their back. The early care of young vampires was observed in a colony of these bats kept in a zoo. Immediately after an infant bat was born, most of the adult vampires clustered around the mother as she clung to the ceiling. They groomed both the mother and baby with their tongues. The baby climbed around on its mother's body and on nearby bats for a few minutes. Then the mother pushed it to a nipple with one wing, and the young bat began to nurse.

When a dish of cow blood was placed in the cage, most of the bats went to feed. The mother bat kept clinging to the ceiling. Another female finished eating, rejoined the mother, licked her face, then regurgitated some blood, which the mother licked up. The mother was fed this way for the following two weeks. Only then did she leave the ceiling and get her own food.

A young vampire relies on its mother for a long time, up to nine months. It nurses milk for about three months. Then the mother begins to give the young-ster blood, regurgitated from her stomach. At the age of five or six months, the young bat clings to its mother's chest and is carried out into the night air for the first time. The mother teaches the young bat how to find food.

One biologist, watching a corral at night, saw a mother bat carrying her youngster land on a horse. With her teeth, she gently removed the scab from a

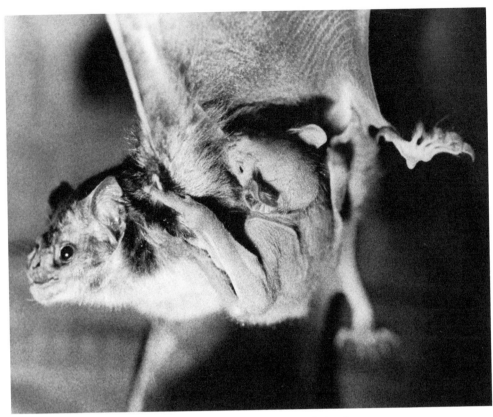

A young vampire bat clings to its mother's body
while nursing milk.

partly healed vampire wound. Then she and her
youngster shared the blood.

If a mother bat dies while her offspring still depends
on her, the youngster is cared for by other bats in the
colony. If the young bat is still nursing, an adult female
adopts it. Within a few days, her milk glands begin to
produce milk and the little bat can nurse.

Long parental care and cooperation within the
colony help ensure that a baby vampire has a good
chance of surviving to become an adult. Human in-

fants need the same kind of care, and usually people feel friendly toward a wild animal, such as the wolf, which has cooperative social behavior somewhat like that of humans. Still, many find it hard to appreciate vampire bats despite the similarity of behavior.

The people who like vampire bats the most are probably those who know them best. Biologists who keep vampires in laboratories have discovered that they become tame and friendly within a few weeks. They can be handled safely without gloves. Dr. Alvin Novick of Yale University had a vampire named Gwendolyn, which hung upside down from his shirt pocket while he worked. Gwendolyn also enjoyed sitting in his hand, and she was greatly missed when she died after spending five years at Yale. (Another vampire survived for nearly thirteen years in captivity, and wild vampires are known to live at least nine years.)

Vampire bats are exceptionally clean animals. If you have ever watched a cat groom itself with its tongue, you can picture a vampire doing the same, except the bat does so while hanging upside down by one foot. With its free foot, the bat scratches every bit of fur and skin it can reach. Then it licks these areas with its tongue. After shifting feet, the bat grooms the rest of its body. Its wings are opened, turned, and twisted until all of their surfaces have been licked. The bat cleans itself as soon as possible after eating or getting soiled. And vampire bats also groom their neighbor's fur as they cluster together in their roost.

A biologist looks into a large hollow tree,
a common roost for vampire bats.

The roosts of vampire bats include caves, buildings, mines, wells, and hollow trees. Colonies of vampires use several roosting places and are made up of twenty to one hundred individuals. A biologist who studied vampire populations in Argentina concluded that the bats were divided into a central colony and several satellite colonies. The central group was led by a dom-

In a colony of vampires, the bats rest close together
and groom one another with their tongues.

34

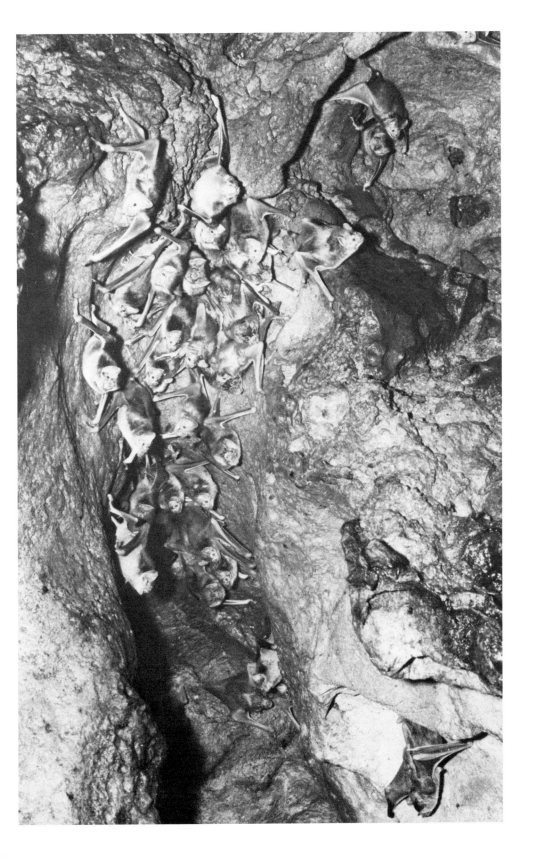

inant "boss" male and included most of the females and some young males. The satellite colonies were almost entirely made up of young male bats. The groups were not rigidly separated, though; there was a lot of visiting back and forth.

From such studies, biologists know that vampire bats have a complex social life. They hope to learn more about it. For good reasons, however, the research emphasis for a long time was on a single part of the lives of these bats: What happens when darkness falls and the vampires leave their roosts to search for a meal of blood?

3

A DIET OF BLOOD

The cattle settle down for the night and lie in a pasture lighted only by stars. They rest comfortably, undisturbed except perhaps for a barely noticeable feeling that a lightweight object has landed on their body or a tiny twinge of pain somewhere on their skin. The cattle shake their heads or flap their ears at these annoyances, then go back to sleep. The dawn light reveals many vampire wounds on them.

A remarkable series of photos by J. Scott Altenbach shows the changing wing positions of a vampire bat in flight.

Vampire bats usually approach a herd of cattle or other prey flying low, two and a half meters (eight feet) off the ground. They circle for a few minutes, then land on a cow's back, on top of its neck, or on the ground nearby. When a vampire approaches its prey on foot, it often stays on the ground and feeds from there. Standing cattle are frequently bitten just above the hoof.

Vampires bite just about anywhere on a mammal's body, but they seem to favor certain body locations for certain kinds of prey. Often they bite dogs and pigs on the nose. Or they may cut nursing sows on their enlarged nipples, which can lead to infection and prevent the flow of milk, causing piglets to die. Human bites are commonly found on the toes and fingers, and sometimes on the ears and lips.

Most prey animals of vampire bats pay little attention to their presence. Usually they are asleep, and stay asleep. A cow or horse may lash its tail or swipe with

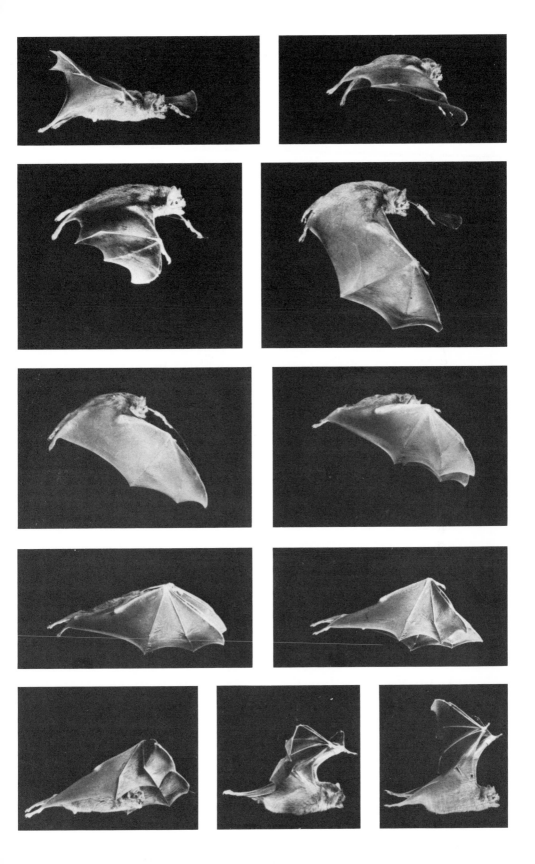

its head at the place where a vampire clings. The agile bat scuttles out of harm's way or leaps into flight, only to return moments later. Mules, however, seem especially sensitive to the presence of vampires. In Trinidad, mules reportedly roll onto their back when they feel a vampire on their skin.

Usually a vampire moves around on the body of its prey for several minutes until it finds a suitable feeding place. Then it licks the site and sometimes shears away hair to get at the skin. Biting with its large, bladelike upper incisor teeth, the bat removes a circular piece of skin, leaving a scoop-shaped wound, three to four millimeters wide. The wound is just one to five millimeters (up to one fifth of an inch) deep. A vampire cannot bite deep enough to tap a major blood vessel such as the jugular in the neck.

A chemical in the bat's saliva prevents the blood from clotting. Blood keeps flowing from the severed capillaries and may seep from the wound long after the bat leaves. This blood, rather than the tiny wound, is what makes vampire bites noticeable in the morning. A rasping motion with the bat's rough-edged tongue also keeps blood flowing or reopens a wound.

Vampire bats are *not* bloodsuckers. They drink blood by lapping, bringing it into their mouth by moving their tongue rapidly in and out. Blood flows to the back of a bat's throat through a channel formed by grooves on the underside of the tongue and on the lower lip.

A vampire bite near the top of this cow's neck
leaves a telltale trail of blood.

A vampire sips blood for several minutes and some-times for more than half an hour. The amount of blood taken is small, though. A bat may drink half its own weight or more of blood, but that is usually only about 30 milliliters (1 ounce). A diet of blood requires a special digestive system. The vampire's stomach is like a long, narrow uninflated balloon until the animal eats. Then the stomach swells until the bat looks like a round ball with wings. Sometimes a vampire gets so bloated with blood that it cannot fly.

41

Blood is a high-protein diet. Vampires digest it quickly and soon begin to rid themselves of liquid waste. They emit dribbles of urine as they feed and for an hour or two afterward. While roosting, they try to avoid getting urine on their fellow vampires.

Although some vampires leave their roost, fill up with blood, and return in just a half hour, many need two hours or more in order to get a blood meal. Several vampires may feed on one prey animal. Fourteen bats were seen on a horse at one time. A steer, dying of rabies, had received thirty fresh bites in one night. Such cases are exceptional, however.

For a time, people thought that the numbers of vampire bats making up a population could be estimated by the number of bites found on livestock or other prey. Now they know that several vampires may take blood from a single wound. This practice saves them time and energy, as the wound may still be oozing blood or can easily be reopened with a bat's teeth or tongue. So the number of wounds is usually fewer than the number of bats that fed from them.

At times biologists have observed puzzling social behavior among feeding vampires. Some bats feed quietly near one another. Some peacefully take turns at a wound. But others defend their meal site—even after they have finished drinking—by making threatening motions and sounds. This variety of behavior may be evidence of the social organization of a vampire population, in which some dominant bats have

42

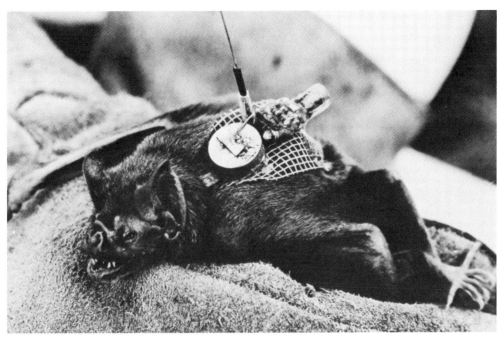
By attaching tiny radio transmitters to vampires, biologists have been able to trace their travels and locate their roosts.

power over others. One biologist has also speculated that a vampire colony may defend "their" cows and drive other vampires away.

Vampire bats hunt during the dark of the night. They are less active when the moon is up and hunt least of all when the moon is full. This difference may be a result of the effects of moonlight on the behavior of their prey. In the tropics, cattle graze and move around on moonlit nights. Vampires prefer sleeping prey. But they can go no longer than three nights without food.

One of the most thorough studies of vampire predation was conducted by Dr. Dennis Turner, who ob-

Dennis Turner looks over Brahma cattle in the morning, counting vampire bites.

served the bats and their prey on a large ranch in Costa Rica. He found no vampire bites on chickens, although 10,000 hens lived in cages without protection from vampires on the ranch. Horse blood seemed to be a favorite food of the bats, but only a few dozen horses were available. The main food source was more than a thousand head of cattle of the Brahma and Brown Swiss-Brahma breeds.

Dr. Turner added the number of bat bites found on the two breeds of cattle and discovered that vampires seemed to prefer the Brown Swiss-Brahma over the Brahma. He wondered whether the bats chose Brown

44

He found more bites on Brown Swiss-Brahma cattle (left) than on the Brahma breed (right).

Swiss-Brahma cows because of their color. Eventually he discovered that the vampire's choice had nothing to do with color, but depended on the behavior of the two cattle breeds.

When a herd composed of both breeds lay down to sleep, the Brown Swiss-Brahma chose the edges of the group. In one herd, he found six young Brahma males that were bitten frequently by vampires. He marked them with greasepaint for easy identification at night, then watched their behavior. Like Brown Swiss-Brahma, these few Brahmas also slept at the edge of their herd. Thus, vampires apparently tend to bite cattle located along the borders of a sleeping herd. It is probably safer and easier for them to approach these cattle.

When vampires head home with bellies full of blood, most of the cattle they leave behind do not necessarily suffer much from their wounds. Some wounds become infected, and bites on cow ears may damage muscles and cause the ears to droop. The occasional loss of an ounce or two of blood does not harm a healthy cow or steer, but heavily bitten animals or livestock that are poorly nourished may lose weight or give less milk. Still, these losses might be forgiven if some vampires did not leave the deadly rabies virus in the sleeping cattle.

4

BAT
CONTROL

Once it was known that some vampire bats carry rabies, Government health and agricultural officials tried to solve the problem in two ways. One was to protect people and livestock from being bitten. People were urged to use bat-proof fencing to keep vampires out of homes, barns, and other buildings. Some corrals were brightly lighted at night to repel the bats. Eventually, antirabies vaccines were developed for cat-

47

tle, but they were expensive, not always effective, and did not stop the spread of rabies from infected bats to other bats. Such efforts were also impractical on many Latin American ranches where cattle roam freely over vast wild range.

Some people tried to solve the rabies problem by killing as many vampire bats as possible. At times, these efforts resembled a war. Shotguns, dynamite, traps, flamethrowers, and poisonous gases were used to kill bats or to destroy their roosts. Hundreds of caves were blown up in Brazil. For a time, the Venezuelan Government's policy was to kill *all* bats within about one kilometer (six-tenths of a mile) of a place where rabies outbreaks occurred.

This war on vampires and their roosts appalled scientists, who had learned that vampires share roosts with many species of harmless or beneficial bats, including those that eat insects. Besides, vampires themselves seemed harmless in some regions, preying lightly on livestock and carrying no rabies. The destruction of caves, hollow trees, and other roosts also harmed other kinds of wildlife.

As the search for an effective means of controlling vampire-carried rabies continued, officials tried to get a more complete picture of the effects of vampires on livestock and people. In 1966, a committee of the World Health Organization of the United Nations called vampire-carried rabies the primary livestock problem in Latin America. The loss was estimated at

48

one million animals a year, at a cost of $350,000,000. In addition, vampires were found to carry the virus of a disease known as equine encephalomyelitis, which kills thousands of horses each year.

At times, outbreaks of vampire-carried rabies practically prevented livestock raising. At a Bolivian ranch one year, the losses were 200 of 1200 cattle, 9 of 70 horses, 18 of 20 pigs, and 25 of 70 goats. The cattle had been vaccinated five times but this measure failed to prevent serious losses.

Vampire bites on humans are much less of a problem, but still occur in some situations. In 1976, for example, a severe drought in a coastal area of Panama caused ranchers to move their cattle inland for better grazing, and vampires near the coast faced a food shortage. Within two months, ninety-five people had been bitten.

No one died, however. Although rabies exists in Panama, only a few isolated cases occur each year. These cases are not caused by vampire bats, scientists believe, and the rabies virus has never been found in Panamanian vampires. Rabies is also scarce or absent in other parts of Latin America. It has never been found in Uruguay, although vampire bats live there and some of those living in neighboring Brazil carry the disease.

Many people in Latin America do not worry about being harmed by vampires. In most ranching areas, bites on humans are unheard of, while in some other

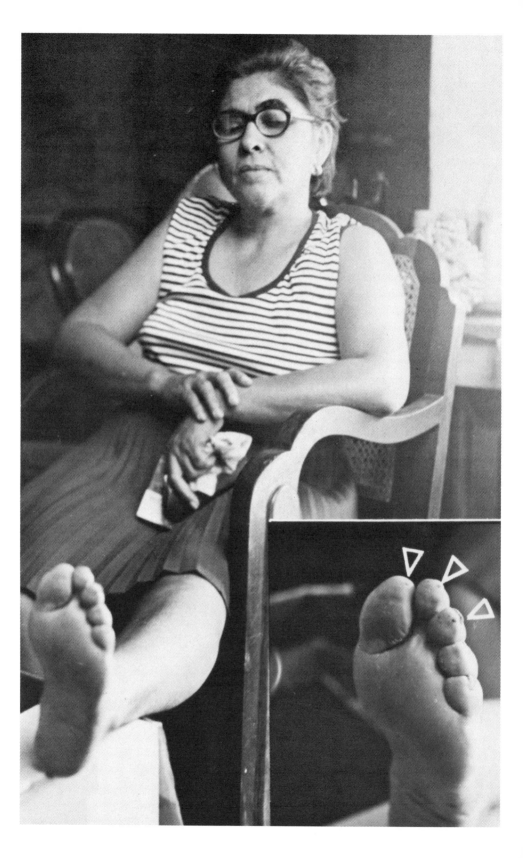

regions generations of people have been bitten but no rabies has occurred. Nevertheless, each year several people in Latin America do die of vampire-carried rabies.

A major research effort on vampire control was launched in 1967. It was supported by the United States Agency for International Development and the Government of Mexico. Laboratory studies were conducted in Mexico and at the United States Interior Department's Denver Wildlife Research Center. By 1971, scientists reported some significant progress.

They had discovered that vampire bats are especially vulnerable to drugs that are used to keep blood from clotting. These anticoagulant drugs had been developed to treat human heart disease. When low doses were given to vampire bats, they died from internal bleeding. Thus, the little bats that need blood for life could be induced to bleed to death.

Scientists figured out two ways to get the drug (whose trade name is diphenadione) to vampires that preyed on livestock. One method involved setting up mist nets near corrals to catch vampires as they approach or leave. A mixture of the anticoagulant drug and a sticky jelly is smeared on their back, and then the bats are released. As usual, the bats begin to clean themselves as soon as they reach their roosts. Other

---

As she slept, this Nicaraguan woman was bitten on her toes by a vampire bat. Arrows point to the tiny wounds.

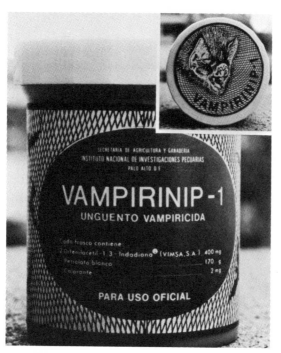

In Mexico, the drug diphenadione, mixed with vaseline,
is called Vampirinip-1 (above).
Whether the drug is spread on the body of a live vampire bat
(top right), which is then released,
or injected into cattle (bottom right),
it is usually fatal to vampire bats that swallow it.

vampires in the colony help lick off the jelly too. In the normal routine of grooming themselves and each other, many bats in a colony receive a fatal dose of the drug. Each bat smeared with the jelly-drug mixture inadvertently causes the death of up to twenty other vampires. In most places where this method has been used, bat bites on cattle drop more than 90 percent.

The second method calls for injecting the anti-coagulant drug into the stomach of a cow. The drug circulates through the bloodstream for a few days but

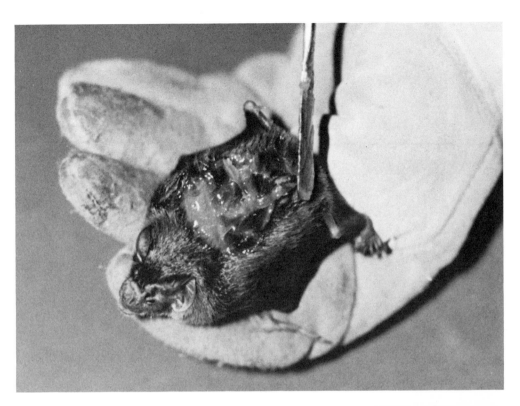

has no apparent ill effects on the cow. If a vampire takes blood from the cow, it receives some of the anticoagulant and soon dies. This method kills only those bats that bite treated cattle, and the drug kills one bat at a time without affecting others in its colony. Both methods of vampire control seem to be harmless to other kinds of bats that share vampire roosts. And both dramatically reduce vampire bites on cattle for several years. They can be repeated if the numbers of vampire bites eventually increase to serious levels.

Both of these techniques are safe, economical, easily applied, and produce quick results. Many Latin American nations now have vampire control programs that use one or both of them. Most of these programs use the anticoagulant drug only in response to outbreaks of rabies among cattle in specific regions. However, a few countries try to kill vampire bats in general, even when rabies may be a minor problem. And sometimes there is still thoughtless slaughter of all bats. In 1974, a Colombian cave was filled with poisonous gas and 2,500 bats of several species were killed.

Such attacks sadden those people who know and appreciate bats. Although biologists are pleased that ways have been found to reduce vampire populations in livestock-raising areas, they oppose efforts to kill all vampires. They are curious to know more about these bats. They want to learn about their complex social life and about how vampires became blood eaters in the first place. Above all, they believe that vampire bats ought to remain as part of the natural community of plants and animals in Latin America.

The vampire bat, after all, is not a mythical monster. It is a fascinating real creature that happens to need blood in order to fly, to raise its young, to live.

GLOSSARY

anticoagulant—any substance that prevents or suppresses clotting (coagulation) of a liquid, especially blood.

echolocation—the ability of an animal to navigate, avoid obstacles, and find prey by means of reflection of sound waves it emits. Dolphins and many kinds of bats have this ability.

encephalomyelitis—a serious, sometimes fatal inflammation of the spinal cord, caused by a virus.

fossils—bones, teeth, whole skeletons, body or leaf imprints, tracks, and other signs of past life that have been preserved in rocks.

predators—animals that kill other animals for food. They include sharks, foxes, robins, and humans, but not vampire bats. Since these bats do not normally kill their host animals as they take meals of blood, they are parasites, not predators.

proteins—complex chemical compounds, made up of amino acids, which occur in all living matter and which are needed for normal growth and maintenance. Amino acids are made up of such elements as oxygen, carbon, hydrogen, nitrogen, and sulfur.

rabies—an infectious, often fatal viral disease of mammals and birds that attacks the central nervous system and is transmitted by the bite of an infected animal. Also called hydrophobia.

regurgitate—to cast up or vomit partially digested food, usually to feed young.

species—a population or many populations of an organism that have characteristics in common, which make them different from individuals of other populations. The members of a species share a common and unique inheritance. They interbreed with each other but not with members of other species.

vaccine—a human-made substance of killed or weakened microorganisms (viruses or bacteria) that are unable to cause serious disease but are able to protect against normal disease-causing microorganisms when innoculated into a human or other animal.

viruses—the smallest, simplest forms of life, which are able to multiply only within the cells of a living thing.

FURTHER READING

Altenbach, J. Scott. *Locomotor Morphology of the Vampire Bat,* Desmodus rotundus. Special Publication Number 6, The American Society of Mammalogists, 1979.

Greenhall, Arthur. "The Biting and Feeding Habits of the Vampire Bat, *Desmodus rotundus.*" *Journal of Zoology,* 168 (1972): 451–61.

Greenhall, Arthur, et al. "Attacking Behavior of the Vampire Bat, *Desmodus rotundus,* Under Field Conditions in Mexico." *Biotropica* 3 (1971): 136–41.

Kaplan, Martin, and Koprowski, Hilary. "Rabies." *Scientific American,* January 1980, pp. 120–34.

Manske, Uwe, and Schmidt, Uwe. "Visual Acuity of the Vampire Bat, *Desmodus rotundus,* and Its Dependence Upon Light Intensity." *Zeitschrift für Tierpsychologie (Journal of Comparative Ethology)* 42 (1976): 215–21.

McNab, Brian. "Energetics and the Distribution of Vampires." *Journal of Mammalogy* 54 (1973): 131–44.

Mills, Richard. "Parturition and Social Interaction Among Captive Vampire Bats, *Desmodus rotundus.*" *Journal of Mammalogy* 61 (1980): 336–37.

Mohr, Charles. *The World of the Bat.* Philadelphia: J.B. Lippincott Company, 1976.

Novick, Alvin. "Bats Aren't So Bad." *National Geographic,* May 1973, pp. 614–37.

Sazima, Ivan, and Uieda, Wilson. "Feeding Behavior of the White-winged Vampire Bat, *Diaemus youngi,* on Poultry." *Journal of Mammalogy* 61 (1980): 102–104.

Schmidt, Karl, and Badger, Daniel. "Some Social and Economic Aspects in Controlling Vampire Bats." *Proceedings of the Oklahoma Academy of Science* 59 (1979): 112–14.

Schmidt, Uwe, and Schmidt, Christal. "Echolocation Performance of the Vampire Bat *(Desmodus rotundus)*". *Zeitschrift für Tierpsychologie (Journal of Comparative Ethology)* 45 (1977): 349–58.

Turner, Dennis. *The Vampire Bat: A Field Study in Behavior and Ecology.* Baltimore: The Johns Hopkins University Press, 1975.

Wimsatt, William. "Transient Behavior, Nocturnal Activity Patterns, and Feeding Efficiency of Vampire Bats *(Desmodus rotundus)* Under Natural Conditions." *Journal of Mammalogy* 50 (1969): 233–44.

Yalden, D.W., and Morris, P.A. *The Lives of Bats.* New York: Quadrangle Books, 1975.

INDEX

*indicates illustration

About the Author

Born in Rochester, N.Y., Laurence Pringle attended Cornell University, where he graduated with a B.S. in wildlife conservation. Later, at the University of Massachusetts, he earned an M.S. on the same subject, and he also studied journalism at Syracuse University. Upon finishing his studies, Mr. Pringle taught high-school science for one year and for seven years was an editor of *Nature and Science,* a children's magazine published at the American Museum of Natural History in New York City. Since 1970, he has been a freelance writer, photographer, and editor. He has three teen-age children and lives in West Nyack, New York.